Full blown orphan

Nick Blundell

For all who, whether named or not, appear within.

Published by Half Moon Books 2019
an imprint of OWF Press Community Interest Company
Otley Courthouse, Courthouse Street, Otley, West Yorkshire LS21 3AN

www.owfpress.com

ISBN 978-1-9993036-9-3

Cover design: Nick Palmer

Acknowledgements

After W.S. Graham was published in Riddled with Arrows Issue 2.3
November 2018

The last stanza of *Rope Bridge* appeared as *Ashes* in Praesepe, Beehive
Poets 2006

.

Printed & bound by ImprintDigital.com, UK

Contents

Quay

Calm today, as the proverbial.
Yet even tranquil water climbs the steps.
As other, harder days, I watch
captivated by the climb of tide,
first tentatively touching the angle of the step,
teasing, testing, taking time,
then over, capturing beyond doubt
and on
to the next one in its reach.
Step by step, tide by tide, season by season.
No end to the pier show.

————————————

I'm on the quay again,
at Holy Island harbour,
the tide slowly climbing the steps.

Last time I wasn't even half an orphan,
now I'm fully blown.

The ebb and flow has carried them away,
yet left me here, both less and more than I was before.

The gulls sound like children.

Boy

As I clamber over rocks,
noticing crabs and tiddlers in pools between,
I'm a boy again
in the long summer holiday
ready for adventure.
Except this time there's no-one to say
careful, mind your step, It's a long way down.

On St Cuthbert's little island
I'm entranced by seals,
and suddenly the tide is in
and I'm rolling up trousers, removing shoes,
wading for the shore.
The battle between embarrassment and delight
ends in easy victory.

The title of this poem is the sound of an elephant's distress call

dealing in
the currency of lifetimes
makes foreign trade difficult
and the exchange rate
hard to calculate

the apocryphal Elephant
squared up to by the Mouse of legend
is panicked not by her opponent's
sinewy tail cheese-wire whiskers
nor even his terrible table manners

her terror comes as she realises
his so-limited longevity
and is made to face
in mouse-shaped miniature
her own pachydermic mortality

this poem ends with the sound of an elephant's distress call
and the squeak of a mouse

Summer

Frailty in one so strong
is hard to look upon.
The one who walks tall and straight
dizzy, bowed down by fever's heat.
The son before the father's weakness
has nowhere safe to fix his gaze.
Past, present, future, meet
in merciless collision.
Childhood's giant lies in Lilliput
with ties of tumour and treatment
pulling, holding down.

Yet even here strength waits
and weakness clinically deceives.
Don't look away in fear from feebled frame,
rather look clear and straight in eyes
with eyes inherited from same.
Strength is not gone but deeper
determination stands the test and more.

Look and be proud,
returning strength with firm resolve.

I see you still

Autumn

Your quietening is hard to hear, and bear,
short not of tales, but breath and time.
Your voice boxed in by frailty,
words weighing less
and more.

Before,
you boomed, flowed, held court,
spoke freely by the hearth.
Now soft,
words saved like sparklers in the autumn night,
you make the packet last.

The silence comes, it hums,
the background noise on which our talking rests.

Yet
your words are heard in thoughts
born not in us but you,
and tales you told, like gold, enfold us still.
We listen.
You cheer, console, affirm,
make clear.
We hear, and hearing,
know you well.

We hear you still.

Winter

Your absence fills the place
though strangely
not with sadness.
Though tears abound
the sound
is not of weeping.
Your quietening complete,
we meet –
take in your silence,
breathe out stories.

We list – names, titles, roles,
the hats you wore
before this time of yielding.

We make our choice –
we will rejoice
and make of this a sharing.

Spring

Ashes ringing the walnut tree
you hold your ground
strangely reluctant to depart.

Each of us passes you
but no clear word is spoken.
All summer quiet whispers
unheard by the others,
the most we grant you.

Through autumn we watch
the breeze diminish you,
hard rain leech your strength,
wild rabbits shadow-chase unknowing
through the sodden smoke ring
which marks your empty breath
under falling leaves.

Soon snow will come and cover,
send us inside.

Bless you

I hear you when I sneeze,
loud, deep, sharp
filling the house with sudden noise.
Bless you.   Bless you.

Mum has given me your handkerchiefs
K in the corner.
I sneeze your sneeze into them,
but they hold my tears.

I'm wearing your shirt,
not quite filling it,
carrying the material I did not choose.
At funerals I wear your coat
(too warm at yours, too soon).
I found a washer in the pocket
and half a cigarette.

I stand in your brown brogues.
Strange, I don't have your height
yet my feet fit your shoes almost.

Kicking them off on an evening
I notice the wear beneath -
marks of your footsteps still
more than mine.

I'm trying to wear them well.
As in a dream I hear you sneeze,
loud, deep, sharp.
Startled I fall safely to your side
not quite knowing you.

Bless you. Bless you. Ah yes.

Do you see me through your tears
I wonder, knowing now.
You put my handkerchief away
and pause.
I see your eyes -
not quite as bright
as I remember.
Your bearing too is heavy -
you carry weight as well as clothes
you did not choose.

I did not want to leave you all
but time had come
and breath was done. No more.
No more.

Remember when
the child in you first rode,
not knowing I'd let go
until you turned -
that yell, excitement clanging like the bell
you rang in triumph?
You could ride!

Ride now, stride out in shoes
I'm pleased to see you wear,

no need to turn.

Yesterday

Yesterday, you hugged and held
and made us welcome,
laughed loud and long,
and told your tales.

The day before you had the answer to our questions,
the experience to find a way to mend,
to make things work.

A few days past you planned and planted gardens,
worked with wood,
then filled your chair and drank your tea,
talking of test matches and tournaments.

A week ago, you revelled
in the sparks that flew,
the tensions you creatively
engendered with your fellows,
and we looked on,
raised eyebrows never overruled a smile.

Just days ago you lived.
Just days ago you died
with us around you
holding and releasing.

Seasons have turned.
From summer's dying
the autumn golds have grown,
only for winter's fingers
to pick them clean
and wipe the earth.
Spring's greens have come,

filled out with sun and rain
till summer's here again.

A year is passed
and long ago you lived.

St Paul's, New York City

And still you stand,
grace place
where face to face
with loss and anger
and empty space
too huge to measure
still you stand

for life in death
and hope through dust
and care for neighbour,
you dare to trust
tomorrow's dawn.

And here you share
with gentle prayer
and tender care
this holy dare –
you challenge all
who saw the fall
who know the cost
of human loss
so well
who've been to hell
and back again

to ring the bell
time and again
five peels, four times –

remember those who fell
but do not dwell in darkness

breathe in the light
the promise echoing round the site
that hope will not be broken.

Seeing stars

with open eyes
and no suspicion of violence

with unboxed ears
and no sound or clamour

with mind made whole
and only an echo of brokenness

with ascending spirit
and no fear of falling

you look into the dark night
and see stars.

Eagle in flight[1]

The sculptor found an eagle
and released her.
She had been soaring unseen,
held by the tree in which she dwelt.

Unimagined until the sculptor saw.

He chiselled away the wood
containing her
exposing her form, feathers, flight.

Then he let her go.

in the gap between the vicissitudes of circumstance and grammar
the poem had been marking time

Unnoticed until the poet heard.

She teased away
superficial stanzas and extraneous syllables
whittling words until truth breathed.

Then she let it go.

---

[1] Eagle in flight', carved by Paul Clarke in woodland at Parceval Hall, Yorkshire
Dales.)

After W.S. Graham

...His job is Love
Imagined into words or paint to make
An object that will stand and will not move.[2]

The paradox of flowing fluid stuff,
   now fixed, fastened into place, constrained.
I cannot think of love bereft of breath,
   to bind in print or frame must be to maim –

to crush the life.

Imagination must be the hinge to this,
first artist's, glimpsing truth along the path
and setting snare in place and time precise
to catch the creature in a trap of glass –

the object stands.

But now another's heart imagines out –
   the one who comes to view the captured beast,
   who sees its lines, and hears its colours shout,
who runs with it, to join it in the feast –

here is the life.

The object stands, it does not move, it is caught well,
yet sparks delight, like children freed from school with all to tell.

---

[2] from *The Thermal Stair*, by W.S. Graham.

Holiday Snap

I saw my face today
under a ridiculous straw hat
chin on the edge of a swimming pool
eyes smiling into the Ionian sun.
The photograph was taken seven days ago.

My Grandpa died when I was twelve.
He drove his car badly and chuckled a lot.
I saw his face today
under a ridiculous straw hat
chuckling at his grandson.

My father died a year ago.
He smoked too many cigarettes but told good stories.
I saw his face today,
chin on the edge of a swimming pool,
eyes smiling at his ageing son.

The photograph was taken seven days ago.
I saw my face today.

Working men

Grandpa juggled bricks and handled mortar as if icing a cake
though his hands and language were calloused,
his heart was soft.

Grandad moved flour in and out of silos
like huge hourglasses. His hair, and lungs
as it turned out, were gluten-flecked.

Dad draughted bits of boats with steady hand,
then managed dye and dirt
in fug of smoke for years.

Three working men
whose bodies bore the marks of industry and toil
in death as life.

When work for me is listening
and telling hope-filled tales –
I get off light.

Sand

and all the time the sand flows through
grain after grain before his eyes
nothing changes, nothing is new

he feels the weight of years, as you,
both caught in place, no way to rise
and all the time the sand flows through

now and again he tries to do
acts out of place, which cause surprise –
nothing changes, nothing is new

you stand against the flow, you too
seek ways to startle, energise
and all the time the sand flows through

the end of it draws into view
he dares to dream - escape, no ties –
nothing changes, nothing is new

each tiny grain a prism of lies
not the whole beach will make him wise
and all the time the sand flows through
nothing changes, nothing is new

ante natal

sixty-eight years from now
on a wednesday
an embolism will choke his life away.

fifty-seven years
a friday
a platinum timepiece will honour long service

forty-four years
another friday
the one he thinks is constant will prove to be other

thirty-two years
a tuesday
his best day will begin and end with a midwife's condemnation

twenty-one years
a thursday
he will graduate with a degree he will believe undeserved

twelve years
sunday
his father's watch will be given him by a man with tear-filled eyes

five years
a monday
he will sit in a classroom with his mother's kiss like a wound on his
    cheek

in a week
it will be wednesday
gloved hands and forceps will pull him into light

but now
this wednesday
he waits, unknowing, undamaged, unknown.

Wind break

For almost a hundred Corfiot summers,
Spiros walked the beach
collecting warm coins from those
who lay upon his sunbeds
and lazed below his gaudy parasols.
Strong and dark as well-carved olive wood,
he was eternal.

With minimum fuss and classic dignity,
one night he died.

They gave him rest high on the hill,
the corner plot within Santa Barbara's bleached walls.
They marked his place with marble,
visiting on saint's days,
with flowers in alabaster vases.

The day we called, after the storm,
the vases lay wind-broken.
We gathered up the pieces and paid our due.

Rope Bridge

It's not the steps that worry me
but the gaps in between,
and the wear of the rope
and the strength of the wind.

It's not the days that trouble me
but the nights in between,
and the weight of my thoughts
and the wind turning the bin over, outside.

It's not your words that harry me
but the silences between,
and the depth of your bitterness,
a howling gale behind a triple-glazed window.

At your request
I burned my bridges, one by one.
And then you told me
you needed someone who didn't
smell so much of smoke.

Grounding

Even though you were scarred
by the manner of his death,
and more so by the cruelty
of those who should have cared,
your father would be proud.

Even though your heavy-handed childhood
and the pressure to confess to sins
you didn't own or comprehend
has damaged you, you would
still be up there in his eyes.

Even though you never will break through
the bitter wall of righteous anger
against those who claim to serve,
you channel fire and fury where it's due
and let your outrage work

Even though you may never understand
how that travesty of faith
is the antithesis of mine,
can we walk on hand in hand
and so disturb some common ground?

Fifth

Eight swans fly south, passing the island to the east, over the sea,
single file, four then four, as if leaving room for another, between,
the fifth of nine, the one who is not there.

They make good speed, rising or falling to find least resistance, best
    wind,
not slowed, it would seem, by the absent place, by the space left,
the fifth of nine, the one who is not there.

For the first four their course is clear and on they go, strong wings
beat time and carry them beyond
the fifth of nine, the one who is not there.

It is the fifth of eight, the sixth of nine, who holds the distance, minds
    the gap,
measures in mind's eye the vacant berth, and follows for them all
the fifth of nine, the one who is not there.

Clearance

The carpet's pile told a story.
Loud in places, shouting,
where heavy furniture
had thought it would stay for ever.
Quieter elsewhere, whispering, hinting,
shape and flow suggesting
movement, life.

In a corner, four clear, curved indentations,
used to holding a particular chair.
In front of them the marks of her feet, soft slippered,
making their bid to evidence the life lived in this room.

He plugged the Dyson in.

Cha-cha-cha

I woke this morning dreaming about Mum,
and thinking that I should call her,
feeling guilty that it's been a while,
particularly now she's on her own.

In the dream we bumped into each other
at a church fete
and she asked me to cha-cha-cha,
then remembered I don't dance.

I woke too soon to tell her she was wrong,
that the cha-cha is in my repertoire.

If I could tell her about the dream
she would smile.

A little while

The house is old, the trees are bare[3]
and all the residents are gone.
Although the Shieling is still there
its range is cold, its day is done.

The one who spoke is silent now,
no booming out from by the hearth,
and she who bore the brunt somehow –
silent in life, so too in death.

Yet we three carry the smouldering coal
and in our voices is echo heard.
Whether mortal or everlasting soul
there is life in common memory stirred.

So close your eyes and listen clear,
see the lights and hear the laughter,
feel the ones who would draw near –
they come, they come, it is hereafter.

---

[3] *From Emily Bronte,   A little while, a little while*